This book belon......................................

D1494717

Silly Races and Other Stories

How this collection works

This *Biff, Chip and Kipper* collection is one of a series of four books at **Read with Oxford Stage 1**. It is divided into two distinct halves.

The first half focuses on phonics-based reading practice, with phonics activities in *Kipper's Alphabet I Spy* and *Chip's Letter Sounds*.
The second half contains three stories that use everyday language: *Get On, Who Can You See?* and *Silly Races*. These stories help to broaden your child's wider reading experience. There are also fun activities to enjoy throughout the book.

How to use this book

Find a time to read with your child when they are not too tired and are happy to concentrate for about ten minutes. Reading at this stage should be a shared and enjoyable experience. It is best to choose just one story or phonics activity for each session.

There are tips for each part of the book to help you make the most of the activities and stories. The tips for reading on pages 6 and 28 show you how to introduce your child to the phonics activities.

The tips for reading on pages 50, 62 and 74 explain how you can best approach reading the stories that use a wider vocabulary. At the end of each story you will find four 'Talk about the story' questions. These will help your child to think about what they have read, and to relate the story to their own experiences. The questions are followed by a fun activity.

Enjoy sharing the stories!

Authors and illustrators

Kipper's Alphabet I Spy, written by Kate Ruttle & Annemarie Young, illustrated by Alex Brychta

Chip's Letter Sounds, written by Kate Ruttle & Annemarie Young, illustrated by Nick Schon

Get On written by Roderick Hunt, illustrated by Alex Brychta

Who Can You See? written by Roderick Hunt, illustrated by Alex Brychta

Silly Races written by Roderick Hunt, illustrated by Alex Brychta

OXFORD
UNIVERSITY PRESS

Great Clarendon Street, Oxford, OX2 6DP, United Kingdom

Oxford University Press is a department of the University of Oxford. It furthers the University's objective of excellence in research, scholarship, and education by publishing worldwide. Oxford is a registered trade mark of Oxford University Press in the UK and in certain other countries

Silly Races, Get On, Who Can You See? text © Roderick Hunt 2005, 2006
Kipper's Alphabet I Spy, Chip's Letter Sounds text © Kate Ruttle and Annemarie Young 2011
Silly Races, Get On, Who Can You See?, Kipper's Alphabet I Spy illustrations © Alex Brychta 2005, 2006, 2011
Chip's Letter Sounds illustrations © Nick Schon and Alex Brychta 2011

Silly Races first published in 2005
Get on, Who Can You See? first published in 2006
Chip's Letter Sounds and *Kipper's Alphabet I Spy* first published in 2011

This Edition published in 2018

British Library Cataloguing in Publication Data
Data available

ISBN: 978-0-19-276415-7

10 9 8 7 6 5 4 3 2 1

Paper used in the production of this book is a natural, recyclable product made from wood grown in sustainable forests. The manufacturing process conforms to the environmental regulations of the country of origin.

Printed in China

Acknowledgements

Series Editors: Annemarie Young and Kate Ruttle

Contents

Phonics

Stories for Wider Reading

OXFORD

UNIVERSITY PRESS

Phonics

Tips for reading *Kipper's Alphabet I Spy*

Children learn best when reading is relaxed and enjoyable.

- Tell your child they are going to help Kipper play 'I spy'.
- For each left-hand page, introduce the alphabet letter by saying its sound clearly, for example, make the sound of 'b' as in *bat*. Don't say 'bee' or 'buh'.
- Ask your child to trace the letter with their fingers while repeating the letter sound.
- Then ask them to 'spy' objects on the opposite page starting with the letter.
- Ask them to say what the objects are, and repeat the word slowly, emphasising the sound of the initial letter.
- Give lots of praise as your child plays the game with you.
- Do the animal tracks puzzle on every page and the maze on page 26.

Have fun!

Match the animal tracks on each left-hand page to one of the creatures on the right-hand page.

This story introduces the letters and sounds of the alphabet:

a b c d e f g h i j k l m n o
p q r s t u v w x y z

For more activities, free eBooks and practical advice to help your child progress with reading visit **oxfordowl.co.uk**

6

Kipper's Alphabet I Spy

d

Play 'I spy' with Kipper.

I spy with my little eye, something beginning with...

apple, ant, Biff, banana, ball, cat, candle

dinosaur, duck, egg, elephant, Floppy, feather

goose, goat, gate, hair, hat, horse, insect

j

k

l

jelly, jigsaw, Kipper, key, kangaroo, ladybird, lion

moon, monkey, milk, nose, nail, net

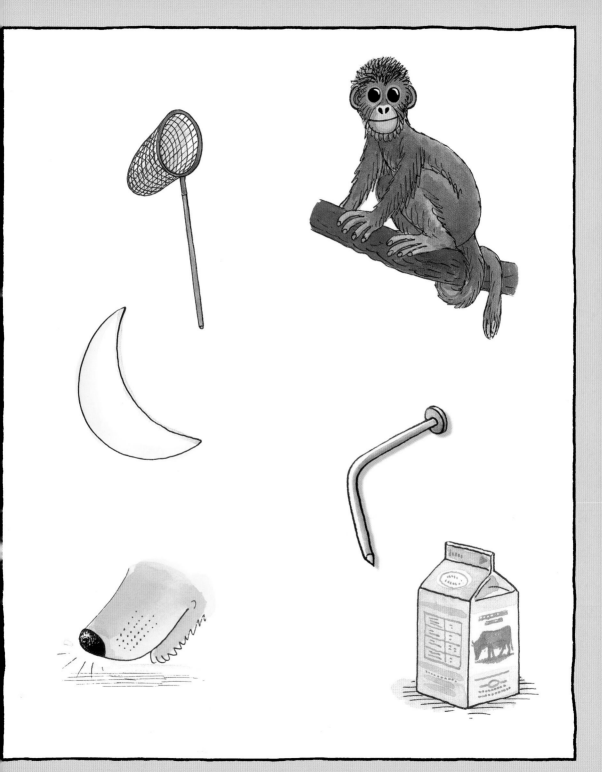

orange, octopus, pear, penguin, purple, queen, quilt

red, rabbit, rainbow, sandwich, sun, tiger, teddy, t-shirt

umbrella, under, volcano, violin, watermelon, watch

fox, box, yellow, yo-yo, yawn, zebra, zigzag

A maze

Help Kipper get to Floppy.

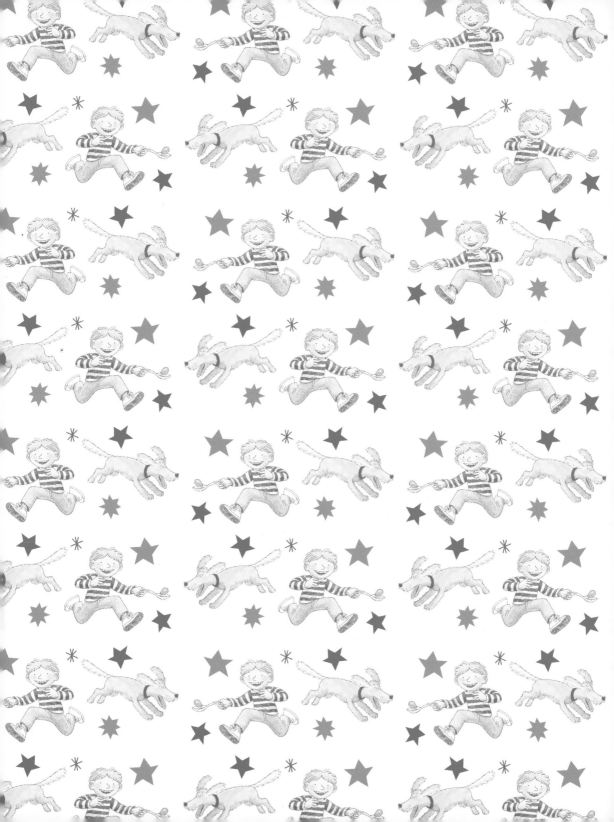

Tips for reading *Chip's Letter Sounds*

Children learn best when reading is relaxed and enjoyable.

- Tell your child they are going to help Chip play 'I spy'.

- For each left-hand page, introduce the alphabet letter by saying its sound clearly, for example, make the sound of 's' as in *sun*. Don't say 'ess'.

- Ask your child to trace the letters with their fingers while repeating the letter sound.

- Then ask them to 'spy' things on the opposite page which begin with that letter sound. Look for lots of words!

- From page 36 enough letters have been introduced to make whole words. Read the 'word trail' with your child. Sound out each word, then say the word (e.g. *p-i-n, pin*).

- Do the odd one out puzzle on each page and the tangled lines activity on page 48.

Have fun!

Find the odd one out on every left-hand page.

This story practises these letter sounds:

s a t p i n m d g
o c k ck e u r h
b f l ff ss

For more activities, free eBooks and practical advice to help your child progress with reading visit **oxfordowl.co.uk**

Chip's
Letter Sounds

Find the sounds
and words in
the pictures.

Trace the letters.
Say the sound.

sun, sea, sand, sandwiches, socks, sandals,
spade, seagulls, sandcastle, straw, sails

Look for ten things in this picture that begin with **s**.

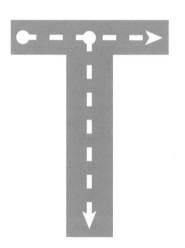

table, teapot, tray, towels, tent, train, tools, tractor, tennis racket/ball, tail

33

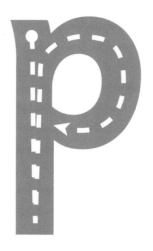

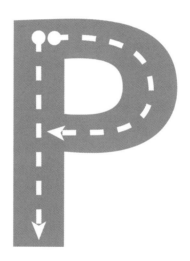

presents, paints, picture, penguins, parrot, panda,
polar bear, pop, pin, parents, pen

Point to all the things at my party that begin with **p**.

Say the sounds and then say the words.

s i t　　p a t

ill, ink, insects, apple, ambulance, ant, animals,
bat, fan, hat, man, lamp, pat, rat, cat, fin, pillow

What things can you find in the picture that begin with **a** or **i**?

Can you find anything with **a** or **i** in the middle of the word?

m M

n N

Say the sounds and then say the words.

m a n   p i n   n e t

night, necklace, newspaper, needle, net, moon,
Mum, mug, mice, monster, monkeys

Look for all the things in the picture that begin with **m** and **n**.

Say the sounds and then say the words.

d o g   D a d   g a p

game, garden, green, girl, grass, goal, goldfish,
Dad, dinosaur, doll, dog, octopus, oranges

c C

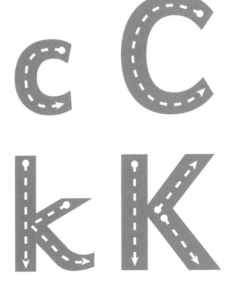

k K

e E

Say the sounds and then say the words.

p a n   m o p

e gg   s o ck

cake, cook, caterpillar, competition, cat, car, castle, crown,
cream, crocodile, cup, kangaroo, kitchen, eggs, elephant

Dad and I have entered a cooking competition. How many things can you find in the picture that begin with **c, k** or **e**?

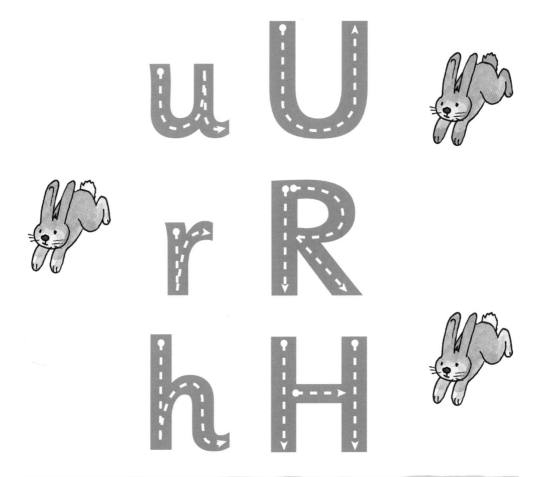

u U

r R

h H

Say the sounds and then say the words.

h o p   m u g

r u b   r o ck

umbrella, rain, red, rabbit, river, rocks, holiday, head, hat, house,
horse, hop, hair, hug, rub, Mum, mug, tree trunk

How many things can you find in the picture that begin with **u, r** or **h**? Can you find anything with **u** in the middle of the word?

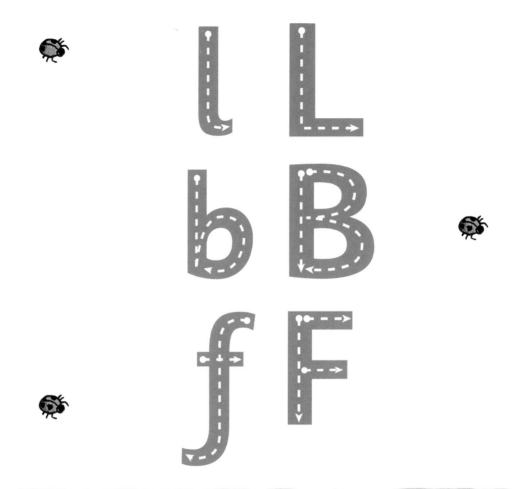

Say the sounds and then say the words.

l e g   b i n

B i ff   m e ss

lady, lolly, leaf, litter, ladybird, flower, bee, butterfly, bench,
bin, biscuit, baby, buggy, balloon, bag, buildings

Tangled lines

Follow the lines to find the objects.

Stories for Wider Reading

Tips for reading the stories together

These three stories use simple everyday language. Encourage your child to read as much as they can with you. You can help your child to read any longer words, like 'spaceman' and 'orange', in the context of the story. Children enjoy re-reading stories and this helps to build their confidence and their vocabulary.

Tips for reading *Get On*

- Talk about the title and look through the pictures so that your child can see what the story is about.
- Read the story to your child, placing your finger under each word as you read.
- Read the story again and encourage your child to join in.
- Give lots of praise as your child reads with you.
- Talk about the story.
- Do the fun activity on page 60.

After you have read *Get on*, find the shell in each picture.

This story includes these useful common words:

get   on   got   and

For more activities, free eBooks and practical advice to help your child progress with reading visit **oxfordowl.co.uk**

Get On

Get on.

Get on, Biff.

Biff got on.

Get on, Chip.

Chip got on.

Get on, Kipper.

Kipper got on.

Oh, no!

Talk about the story

Where was the family?

Who got on first?

Why did the children all fall off?

What do you like to do at the beach?

A maze

Help Biff and Chip get to the sea.

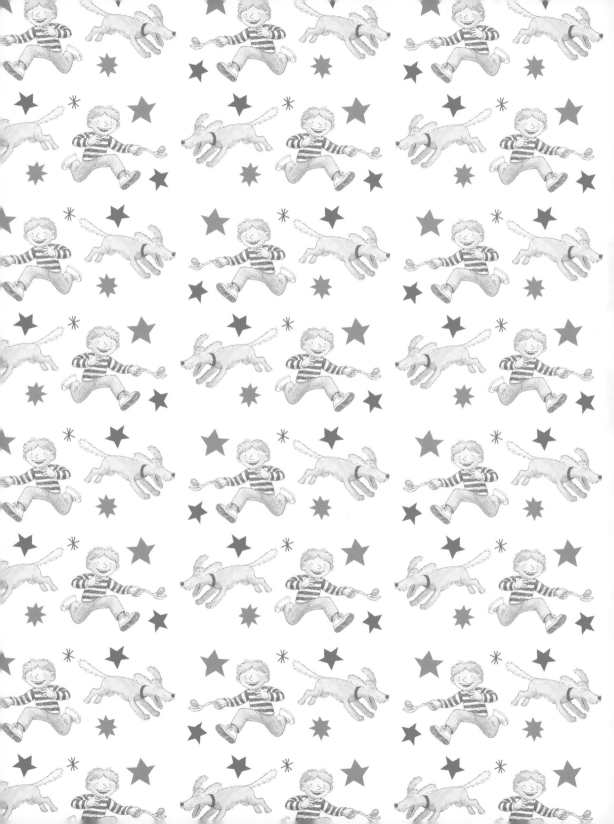

Tips for reading *Who Can You See?*

- Talk about the title and look through the pictures so that your child can see what the story is about.

- Read the story to your child, placing your finger under each word as you read.

- Read the story again and encourage your child to join in.

- Give lots of praise as your child reads with you.

- Talk about the story.

- Do the fun activity on page 72.

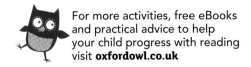

For more activities, free eBooks and practical advice to help your child progress with reading visit **oxfordowl.co.uk**

Have fun!

Who Can You See?

Who can you see?

Biff...

...and Chip.

Mum…

...and Kipper.

Floppy…

...and a spaceman.

No. It is Dad!

Talk about the story

Where was the family?

What shape did Chip make with his hands?

What was Dad wearing?

Which shapes can you make with your shadow?

Match the shadows

Can you match the shadows to the characters?

Tips for reading *Silly Races*

- Talk about the title and look through the pictures so that your child can see what the story is about.

- Read the story to your child, placing your finger under each word as you read.

- Read the story again and encourage your child to join in.

- Give lots of praise as your child reads with you.

- Talk about the story.

- Do the fun activity on page 94.

Have fun!

After you have read the story,
find the bird hidden in every picture.

This story includes these useful common words:

an   got   ran   Dad

Silly Races

Kipper got a banana!

Kipper ran.

Kipper got a banana.

Mum ran.

She got an apple.

Biff and Chip ran.

Finish

They got an orange.

Dad ran.

Floppy ran.

Oh no! Dad fell.

Dad got a duck!

Talk about the story

Why are they silly races?

Which race do you think is the funniest?

Which of the races would you like to be in?

What other sorts of races do people do?

Spot the difference

Find the five differences in the two paddling pools.

Remembering the stories together

Encourage your child to remember and retell the three stories in this book. You could ask questions like these:

- Who are the characters in the story?
- What happens at the beginning of the story?
- What happens next?
- How does the story end?
- What was your favourite part of the story? Why?

Story prompts

When talking to your child about the stories, you could use these more detailed reminders to help them remember the exact sequence of events. Turn the statements below into questions, so that your child can give you the answers. For example, *What goes Dad suggest that the children go on? Who gets on OK first?*
And so on …

Get On

- Dad suggests the family go on a banana boat.
- Biff gets on OK.
- Chip gets on OK.
- Kipper gets on OK.
- Then they all fall off!

Who Can You See?

- Biff and Chip are making shadows in the tent.

- Chip makes a dog shadow with his hands.

- Mum and Kipper are swatting a fly.

- Floppy sees a spaceman.

- It's OK, it's only Dad!

Silly Races

- The children run an egg and spoon race. Kipper wins a banana.

- Mum and Dad run a sack race. Mum wins an apple.

- Mum and Dad and Biff and Chip run a three-legged race. Biff and Chip win an orange.

- Mum and Dad run a flipper race.

- Dad falls in the paddling pool!

- What did Dad get?

You could now encourage your child to create a 'story map' of each story, drawing and colouring all the key parts of them. This will help them to identify the main elements of the stories and learn to create their own stories.